LANE'S THEORIES

BY JAMES E. LANE

DORRANCE
PUBLISHING CO
EST. 1920
PITTSBURGH, PENNSYLVANIA 15238

The contents of this work, including, but not limited to, the accuracy of events, people, and places depicted; opinions expressed; permission to use previously published materials included; and any advice given or actions advocated are solely the responsibility of the author, who assumes all liability for said work and indemnifies the publisher against any claims stemming from publication of the work.

Dorrance Publishing Co
585 Alpha Drive
Suite 103
Pittsburgh, PA 15238
Visit our website at *www.dorrancebookstore.com*

ISBN: 978-1-4809-2696-7
eISBN: 978-1-4809-2834-3

EARTH'S CORE/THEORY

A) The Earth's core is a finally efficient furnace. The Earth's oils insulate it and bring down its temperature.

B) The natural gases serve as a pressure equalizer, so when the Earth expands the gases, will contract, as the pressure decreases, the gasses expand. O-core

C) If we keep drilling into the Earth's surface eventually were going to have an atomic blowout.

D) The more gases we remove, the hotter the reactor will get.

E) At some point they more energy we remove the balance point will be broken and game over.

F) We must try to lower the core temperature. Only one or two degrees at this point and we're going to wish we had.

G) Let's start calculating worldwide temperatures and see who needs to work on their program.

H) Tell big energy companies we want them to lower Earth's temperature 1° one every two years. We don't care how you do it, but get it done. After all we do, pay the fuel bills. Add another charge; you'll be able to figure that one out. With that being said, I also include myself in that category. I know it's wrong to abuse our planet, but oh well, everyone else is doing it. What am I supposed to do?

I) Wait a minute, are there others who feel the way I do about the beautiful planet we live on?

J) My guess is there are millions of people who feel in their hearts the same way I do. Stop the abuse now.

K) If you were seeing a member of your family getting abused, would you not step in to help? Some people don't care, those are the minority, those who feel as I do are the majority.

These are the questions we need to be asking ourselves. Now depending on which group, you ask the question to, you will get a different answer.

Environmentalist will tell you, humans are causing irreversible damage.

Big energy companies will tell you everything is just fine. We just need to keep drilling, all over the world.

I just cannot buy into that theory, that everything will be fine. Of course I need to fill my vehicle up with gas and turn on my electric stove.

Without those necessities we would parish from hypothermia, but the problem as I see it is not that we can't go without energy. We are as a race being ignorant and problematic about how we're handling the problem.

Temperature of Earth

Earth is a planet, with a nuclear reactor, setting in the core.

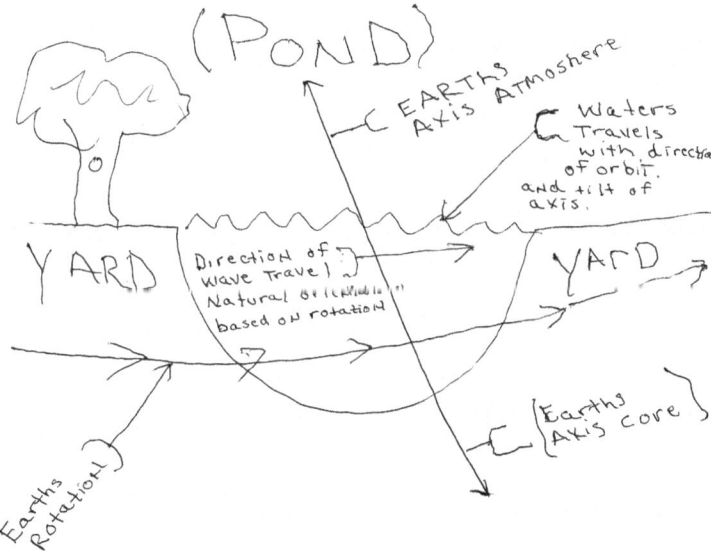

That is a common theory we can all agree on.

Now hear me out, if scientists were handling a nuclear core, the only safe way to do that would be to place they core in a nuclear reactor. Even this is risky. Look at Chernobyl and Three Mile Island. One was everted, one wasn't. Almost happened again in Japan.

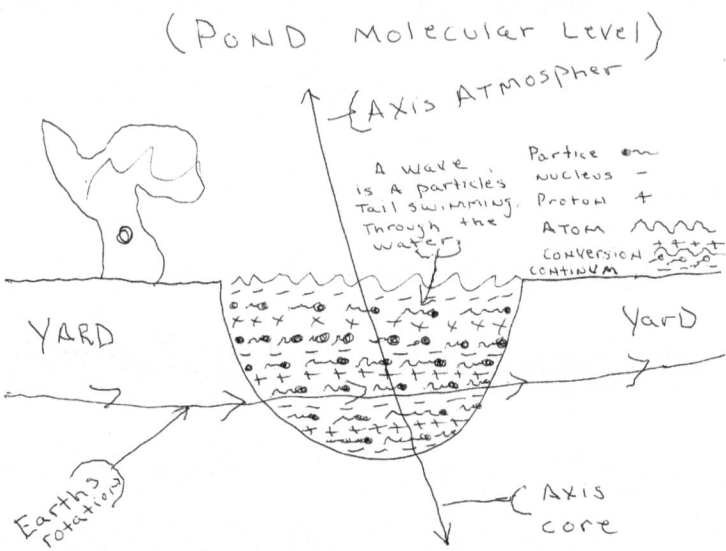

Now does it make sense to keep drilling into the encasement of the Earth's nuclear reactor? Also now using fracture.

At what point does it become unsafe? Also, what would be the first warning signs? Answer: The Earth's temperature would start to rise.

Isn't that the situation we're facing now? Earth's temperature is on the rise.

Is there any explanation for the temperature rising? Is it possible we're doing damage to the natural heat process of the Earth?

Let the nations whose economics depend on oil for their existence be given a share of the development of new energy solar, thermal, dynamic, etc. Whatever their current export values are, they will keep that share. Let's do this fairly. It can be done. We all need to feed our families. The Middle East has beautiful beaches. Let's keep it that way.

Start thinking and start making.

LANE/EARTH CORE THEORY

For once and for all, can we get past the mystic of nature to turn the unpredictabilities into predictable?

Yes, I too love nature. But in reality, there is no nature. Our planet acts as a machine it has processes unbeknownst to us. The human race is but one of its millions of processes.

It is perfectly normal to get wrapped up in the whole nature thing. It soothes us to feel part of something. Unfortunately for the first time in species evolution, the host to our existence is in real threat of becoming extinct.

What our goal should be is sustained mutual fulfillment with our planet. The technology exists, the mindset does not

LANE'S THEORIES

(EARTH'S CORE THEORY)

To gain a proper insight into the mechanical processes taking place on Earth, there is no better place to start than the Earth's core.

They core is as dense as a black hole and can for practical purposes can be said to be one in the same. The difference is the black hole is ignited and occupied.

The planet's core has finally produced enough overburden to protect species from its deadly effects. Systems that allow (cohabitation?) of the planet to evolve.

I must now stray from the common-held view of extinction of species. I do agree that thousands of species have died, plants, animals, and otherwise.

What I think that is important not to overlook is the fact that the core of Earth that produced those species has not stopped functioning.

It is my contention that as long as the nuclear core in the center of Earth continues to burn, any and all previous lifeforms have the ability to reproduce at a later time and climatic period. The chemical DNA markers that were responsible for that species replication the first time can be reproduced in a later timeframe. We shall call this (species reintroduction. Time line).

The Earth's core literally controls the species propagation based on climate factors. It has a DNA bank of thousands of possibilities. When the climate is correct, new species appear and reappear. Based on strict chemical markers. Allow certain DNA to flourish. For the most part species survival is short, comparative to a planet's longevity. Specie health depends on planet health.

When the core of a planet burns out, the planet has finished its lifecycle. No longer having the capability to sustain life because of poor circulation, the old girl goes out to pasture.

As the universe speeds quicker away from the Earth, eventually the distant stars will fade. Gone too far away to see. As the sun burns out, the Milky Way galaxy goes into a frozen, dark, barren infinity. A corpse planet. All planets die. All species die.

They all reappear in succession in the closest new galaxy, and the cycle continues. Chemical transpondence.

The theory of the core is one of the least understood, largely because of its inexistabilty to study.

The core in fact is the live part of the planet. The original genius from the sun from which lifeform comes. All other lifeforms are really overburdened, living in a symbiotic state of give and take.

Acting independently from true nature. It is this behavior that will eventually cause the end to human existence.

However, it will not be they end of the planet. She has a different lifecycle than the species that (inhabit?) her. The planet is independent from its inhabitants.

In the very center of the Earth's core lies the presence of one single atom. It was from that atom the precursor to our modern planet came.

They DNA from that one single atom set up the building block of our Planet Earth. With that process, core building of our planet bonded with the sun's nuclear fusion and fission capabilities.

That single atom is the center of the Earth. They most complex atom of them all. A supernova atom. The strongest atom to survive the sun's vaporizing effects. A spore, if you will.

It is to this atom that other bond particles will soon bond with other particles to form new atoms and start to build compounds of heavy metals. Planet Earth core in formation.

For clarification of following text.

My driver: oil, gas, and mining are affecting Earth's dynamics, heating, and cooling.

(Displacement factor)

100's of millions of gallons of crude oil.

100's of millions of cubic feet of natural gas.

(Replacement factor)

Most logical replacement of lost fuel displacement. Groundwater/seawater.
(Repelling factor)

Oil, as well as gas and pressure, push against the groundwater water/gas
and oil/will not mix. Coefficient bond. As we draw down gas and oil, we take
away the thermal transfer process the Earth's core needs to run efficiently.

If we keep lowering they pressure that holds the nuclear reactor in balance, that is a negative effect. Almost as though the volcanoes have lost their
prime.

We have not experienced the force of a Mount St. Helens in a long time.
That concerns me. What is happening to the energy transfer of North Amer-
ica? No large tremors like the Oakland of the eighties.

Those are horrible tragedies, and I don't ever mean to imply we can't do
without these events. But from a continent in/formation. Isn't it peculiar that
it just stopped happening? The Earth's atmosphere heating up the core seems
to be less forceful than, say, thirty years ago.

As we remove gas and oil, what takes up the volume that mining displaces?
Gas and oil are the main cooling system, for they are Earth's nuclear reactor.

What now if groundwater and brine deposits from drilling? Now that the
oil that you're displacing that normally would hold the water back. What about
the possibility of cooling the reactor?

Would that not contribute to the melting of the icebergs? Heat created
by steam from the reactor being inundated with water.

Why haven't there been any big volcano eruptions lately? Don't you find
that peculiar? They used to occur regularly.

Could it be possible that our intervention could be halting platechtonics?
(Solution)

Take mean temperature on all volcanoes, subduction zones, oceanic, thermal
vents, lava flows. Pattern (thermalcline?) turnovers get a measurement of input
and output. Gain an insight into the core reactor's thermostatical functions.
(Outflows)

Examine the mineral content of lava flows. Look for chemical marker
changes. Primarily we're looking for salinity level changes. If seawater is replacing the core containment area, there should be higher levels of salt in lava flows.
(Smoke)

Monitor lava flows for moisture content. See, if they content, changes as
we get closer in orbit to the sun.
(Compression Factor)

The Earth releases more energy as it approaches sun on its orbit. Where does the energy go? Does Earth need to release more energy to the poles to keep them frozen?

(Freeze versus Heat)

If the cores, they are mechanism for thermal heat. Would not the icebergs of the poles not be the thermal cold?

(Two Forces Working as One)

Icebergs melting

Thermal reactor-flooding. Heat steadily climbing.

(Forecast)

Ugly to medium ugly.

(Core Simmer)

As Earth's nuclear reactor continues to warm up. Oil industries keep removing Earth's only cooling properties.

Crop failures are the end result of long-term temperature increases. No wheat, rice, or raisins for our bellies. No feed for our livestock. A hot desert-like environment void of life. Billions of years of (dissonant?) isolation in our planet's future. Finally we have killed our mother. Rest in peace, beautiful. I will miss your blue and white sunny disposition. Sorry we had to leave you so drab. And distraught. People always hurt the ones they love. Sorry, my bad.

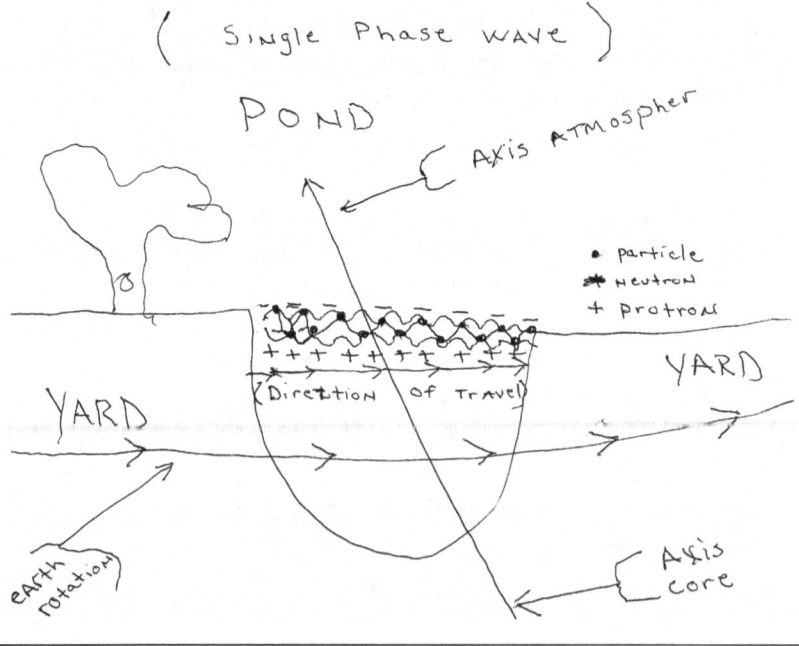

Volcanoes must continue to erupt to get rid of Earth's heat.

No correct me if I'm wrong but does it make sense to frack the ground for gas. The gas does not want to rise so were going to blow it out of the ground. The Earth has way more sense than are E.P.A. has, I'd say.

If I had a glass that was cracked, I would throw it in the trash before I cut my lip on it.

Is the coal mine in Pennsylvania still on fire? Maybe you might not want to frack in that area.

Can anyone answer this question for me? Why? Is it not enough to wait for the gas to rise on its own, then your company is only doing 1/10 of the damage?

You're already charging me $3-whatever a gallon? How about 4 dollars a gallon and we'll wait for it to come up? How's that? Impatient ones. Quit risking my nation's future on your whim. Get out of Ohio and go back to where you came from. I love my state. And you can't do this no longer. It is unacceptable, unethical, and unhuman.

Use existing technologies until we can switch over. We must establish a timeline. Now.

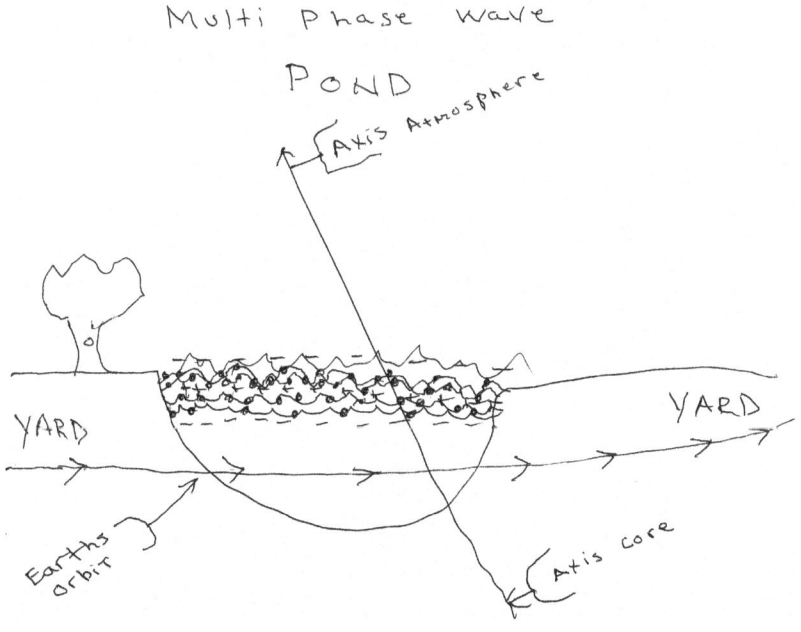

Then it's just a matter of giving Earth time to heal and restart the platech-tonic process. If the volcanoes return to activity, we'll take that as a good sign.

Used oil needs to go back in the ground from which it came. Although it will be diluted and burned, it will still contain the primary thermal properties needed to cool the reactor. Just replacing engine oil alone will mean millions of gallons a year going back into the Earth.

Then allow the Earth to clean the viscosity level of the newly added oil through the heat and mineral heat transfer process. By burning out the impurities which the Earth has the process mechanics to do and turning the water into carbon while providing a safe place to do it. The caverns and lakes from which it came, a natural refinery.

After so much of a timeframe, the oil will be able to be drawn for use again while still serving original intent.

EARTH'S CORE THEORY

Let's talk about life on Earth and what it means to be part of our planet's co-habitational process that we currently call nature.

I want to make a distinction here at this juncture. We don't live in nature. We are nature. Just as much as the plants and animals that we call wild. We in our infinite knowledge call our coinhabitants wild. Who are we? We are the wild ones. Out of control, I would say.

As part of an ecosystem, species have rules to follow. And since no one seems to know the rules, I will attempt to spell them out for you.

It is our function to cohabitate with the planet's environments, not to singlehandedly dismantle them.

Okay, now it's not your fault because you didn't know the rule. You are all forgiven and are being let off with a warning. One giant do-over.

Now I guess at this point you're asking yourself, what can I do? When that answer comes to you, start acting upon it. If enough people follow your lead, you might be on to something. It's better than sitting back and not doing anything. (Get on the bus, Gus. Make a new plan, Stan. Don't need to be coy, Roy, just set yourself free.) Great advice from a musical genius. Apply the advice as you see fit.

Let's eat some roast.

They Earth's core is a fine work of efficiency. It's been running operationally now 4.5 billion years with not one single breakdown. More dependable then a Chevy truck even. The Earth's oil's insulate the core and bring down its temperature. The natural gasses serve as a pressure equalizer. As the Earth expands, they gasses uncontract. As the Earth condenses, so do the gasses.

The more gas and oil that gets removed, the hotter the reactor will become. We are denying Earth its own thermal cooling process.

We need to solve this problem. The core temperature needs to dissipate or the core will burn through prematurely.

For once and for all, can we get past the mystic of nature? There is no guesswork here. We have known for a long time how the core functions.

I am challenging the Tunguska theory. It is said to be the cause of a meteorite exploding over the Earth in near proximity.

Poppycock, I say. All the timber was still lying on the ground. Had it been a meteorite of that magnitude, all the timber would've been vaporized. The soundwave shock may have knocked the forest down. But there would have been evidence of this. (Tinder?) would've been splintered. Not just lying down like a lumberjack's cache. And the blast pattern would've been far more pronounced, with scattered traces of meteorites being found for hundreds of miles around the top of the meteorite, which would blow upward and out. Scattering for hundreds of miles. Yet no evidence was found. I think it was a shear force that moved vertically across North (Amer?). That area may be a hinge point in playtechtonics. It looked like force came from ground, not the sky.

I think we had an Earth anomaly like a (remsisance?) value, underground explosion, nuclear force blast.

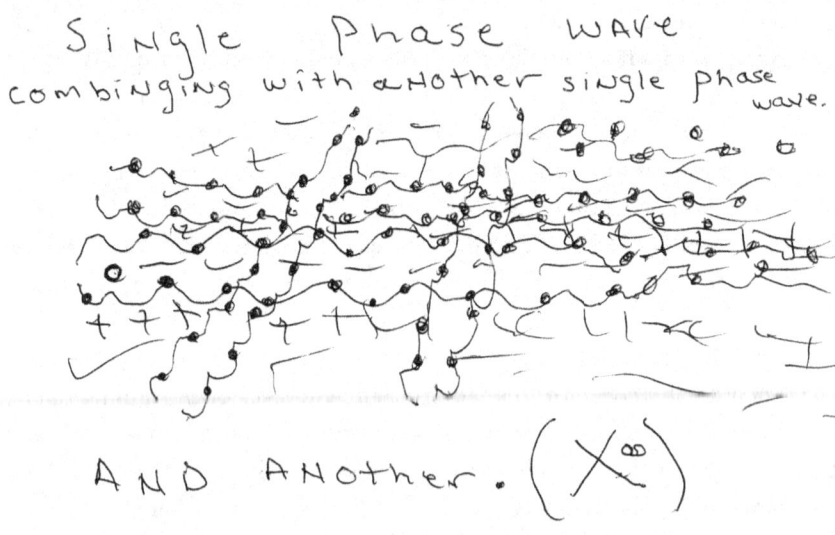

Force spreading outward from its epicenter, making it appear to be struck.

I find it to be a much higher probability that the dinosaurs were poisoned through the water supply. Natural occurrence of the Earth releasing pockets of arsenic and sulfuric acid, which would've been much more in abundance then, in addition to bleach and ammoniation possibilities. Why must we look to outside possibilities such as asteroids? I think Mother Earth is quite apt and capable of specie genocide. She does not need any outside encouragement. She has no emotional attachment to her species. She has no feelings at all. Her reactions are purely mechanical, based on energy availability levels.

Neutrality/Wave Theory

I have always been drawn in by the mesmerizing effects of waves.

For me, waves (are) one of the most energetic emotions known to the human psychology. I can feel it, hear it, taste it, see its visual effects all around me.

The transfers of energy taking place is rejuvenating to the soul. It reconnects me at a primitive level.

I love to stand in the woods and watch and listen as large wind waves flow through the woods, the trees, and shrubs and tall grasses.

Bend, sway, and contort to the rhythm of strong and intermittent wind waves.

The feel you get! On your skin, your face, your hair. It is a feeling of joy and promise. It is our connection to the past. It feels good. Because we belong. Understand your place.

I enjoy watching birds jump up and set their wings into the wind.

And watch the birds as they quickly move out of sight. Moving at breakneck speeds. Far surpassing their physical abilities.

Or watching a large trout as it torpedoes out of its secluded shaded rock.

Into the full sunshine, moving with the speed of a quick downriver current. Again surpassing their physical abilities. By using the Earth's powers to enhance their own abilities. Mind over matter. It appears. If you believe a bird. Brain and a fish understand thermal dynamics. As for me, I am a believer. They seem to know what they're doing.

I now would like to imply that the human anatomy replicates the energy sources of the Earth.

The waves of the ocean are beating at the shores. Just like a human's heartbeats. The oceans also have a pulse. We call it a wave. The wave is the same for humans. If you ever get an electrocardiogram done on your heart, look at the graph. There is your proof.

Humans have waves running through their hearts. And the graph looks just like the waves of the ocean. That's because the same energy source created both. We are systematically entwined. A replication of a replication. All leading back to the Earth's core.

Next we will define what energy is, and then we will discuss how it travels through the process of atom interface.

(Two Types of Energy Waves)

Dark energy and light energy. Both energies work on entirely different principles.

Dark energy is a constant energy. It exists from the center of Earth's core up to the very edge of Earth's stratosphere. It is lost at this point due to loss of strength.

Light energy is not a constant energy. It is a friction-generated energy. Also it extends from Earth's core to the very edge of stratosphere.

Light energy travels through dark energy. For that is the method of travel, a highway of sorts. Without dark energy, light energy would not be able to travel.

Let's think of dark energy as a magnetic force. And light energy as electrical force.

The combined weight of magnetic materials in a planet comprises the total magnetic force of a planet. The force will extend to the outside edge of a planet's atmosphere. Beyond that point, power is lost. Weight-to-distance ratios apply.

Magnetic—all magnetic atoms stay at home. They are codependent atoms. But they do not take or give of themselves. They are an energy of gravity. They simply combine their force. In a sense, the force is controlled by the force it creates. Electrical—atoms share parts and move in unison. Pass energy along and through an area. Atoms do not stay at home. Electrical atoms are also an element of gravity.

The electric-magnetic force equals gravity, acting on objects with the force of an object's resistance to objectivity. If you guide and not conquer such is gravity. The magnetic force stays at home and is not a traveler.

(Dark energy—not visible.) (Light energy—visible.)

Only an overload in electrical energy can be seen, which accounts for a small percentage of visible light.

The only time magnetic light can be seen is during an atomic bomb. Dark energy reassemblance—energy returning to its original state. Dark energy cannot exist in an unnatural state; magnetic can change its own composition by changing its proton arrangement and moving force in the opposite direction.

So magnetic atoms have a property of (bi-polar functionality).

When a nuclear bomb goes off, all wildlife in the ground zero area disappears by converting back to base elements. Reassemulation—they don't actually vaporize. The DNA and the energy are reabsorbed back into our planet, acting on the same mechanical principle as a sponge. Instead of absorbing water, the sponge absorbs heat and converts it back to electromagnetic energy. A constant correction of coversion is continuously at work. It's the way we function. Diatomic reabsorption.

Hard bond = magnetic

Soft bond = electrical

NEUTRALITY FORMULA

A) The ability of waves to move through each other.
B) The waves still remain a particle and a wave.
C) The dynamics of each individual wave remain the same.
D) Temporarily get a gross force as waves combine.
E) You do not numerate combined forces up or down.
F) Nice smooth transfers of energy, all energy waves work on same principle.

Neutrality/Wave Theory
Single Phase Waves

A) Two waves heading straight at each other.
B) Graph
C) Graph
D) Graph
E) Arrows indicate directions of travel.
F) The waves travel in the opposite directions without the particles ever coming into contact with each other.
G) Nice, smooth transfers of energy. All energy waves work on the same principle.

Neutrality/Wave Theory
X3 (Combination Waves)
Work on the same principle.
A) Graph

B) Moving in different directions.
C) Graph
D) Notice point of intersection all particles move through without disruption of flow.
E) There is only a gross force gain at intersection. The three waves still keep their net values.

Wave Theory

When waves stack up, the force of waves can quickly develop new lanes of travel.

Wave Theory

| Date | · | Title | SiNgle Phase wave X 2 |

A) 2 waves heading straight at each other

wave 1   wav 2

particle A1) ● ● ● ●   ● ● ● ●
            ────→   ←────

                wave1   wave 2

wave   B)

How particle
Ocilates
Through
one aNother   C)

wave 1   wave 2

ENd
pass   wave 1   ENter
sectioN   ENC
pass

D) arrows indicate direction of travel

E) the waves travel with out the particles ever comeing in contact with each other.

Priorities

22

Shallow waves are more erratic. Their composition is affected by sea bottom changes in contour effect waves' stability.

Deep waves are long and controlled. The sea bottom loses its effect. Or less effect. Will say.

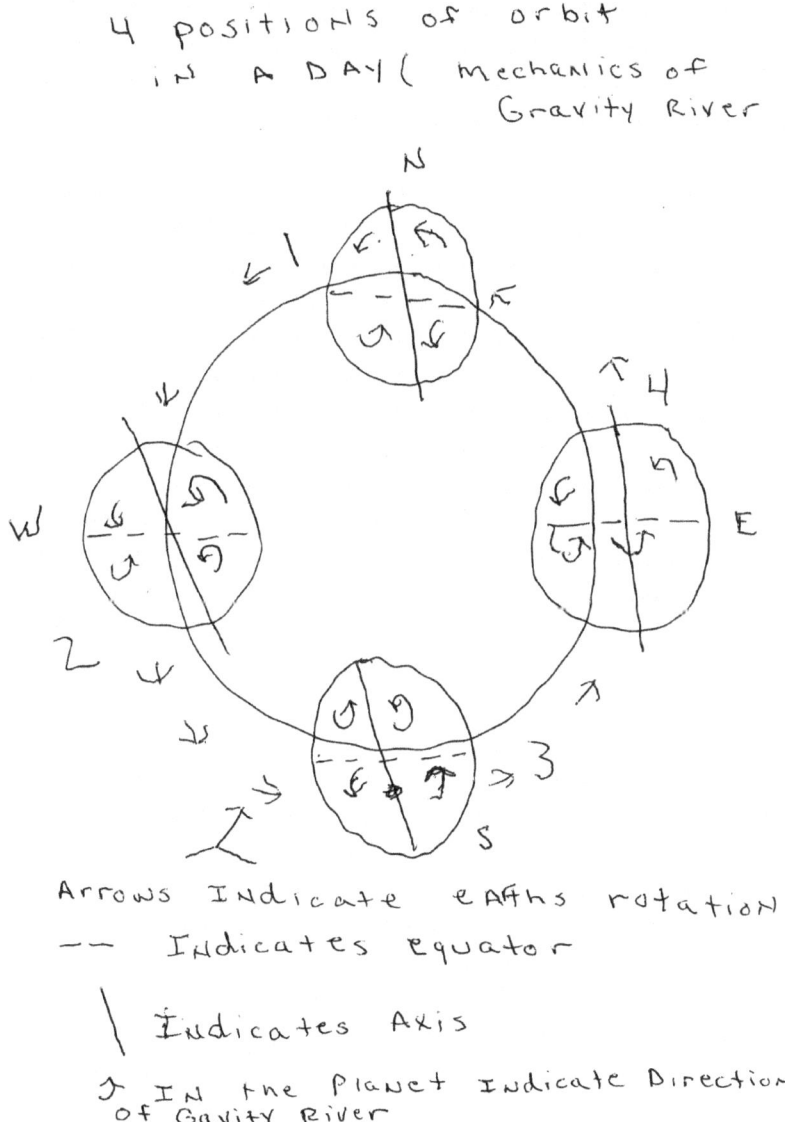

4 positions of orbit in A DAY (mechanics of Gravity River

Arrows Indicate eAƒhs rotation
-- Indicates equator

| Indicates Axis

↱ IN the Planet Indicate Direction of Gavity River

Neutrality

How energy passes through space and atoms.

The particle piggybacks across and through atoms while split polarities travel across the top and bottom of atoms. Reassemblance keeps repeating this process as energy keeps moving one atom at a time.

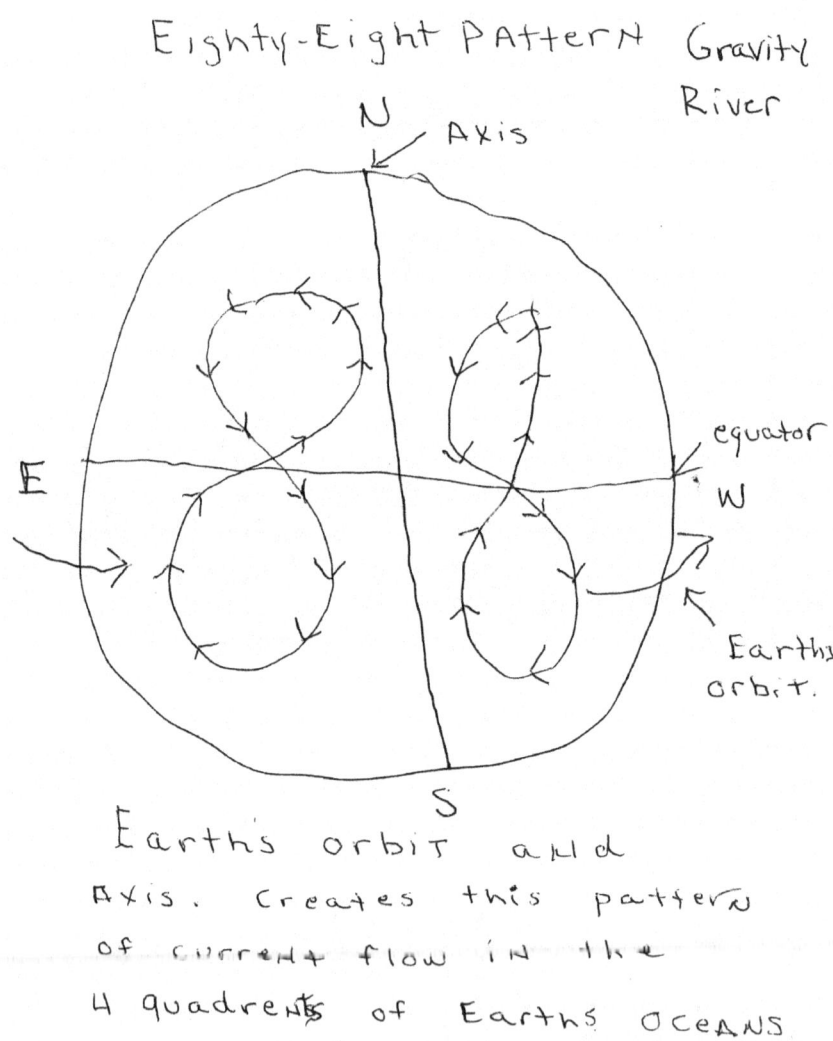

Eighty-Eight PAtterN Gravity River

N Axis

equator
W

Earths orbit.

E

S

Earths orbit and Axis. Creates this pattern of current flow in the 4 quadrents of Earths oceans

Energy can move in a three-dimensional pattern of any combination thereof. That is what gives the atom the ability to build upon each other, while still maintaining original state.

The sum of the whole as well as the whole of the sum. Interchangeable.

Neutrality

Static electricity is a genetic freak that is redirected. You can think of it as a Siamese twin. You can only see the electricity because it is unstable. As soon as static electricity returns to its original state, it goes away. It is a way to keep current flowing. When traffic clears, the energy redisperses.

It is a syncopation of OHMS.

If you look at a cross-section of current, it looks like it is moving vertically to the coast. That is your eyes playing a trick on you. It is a deception of your

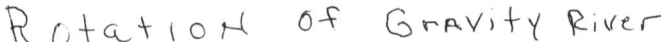

Rotation of Gravity River

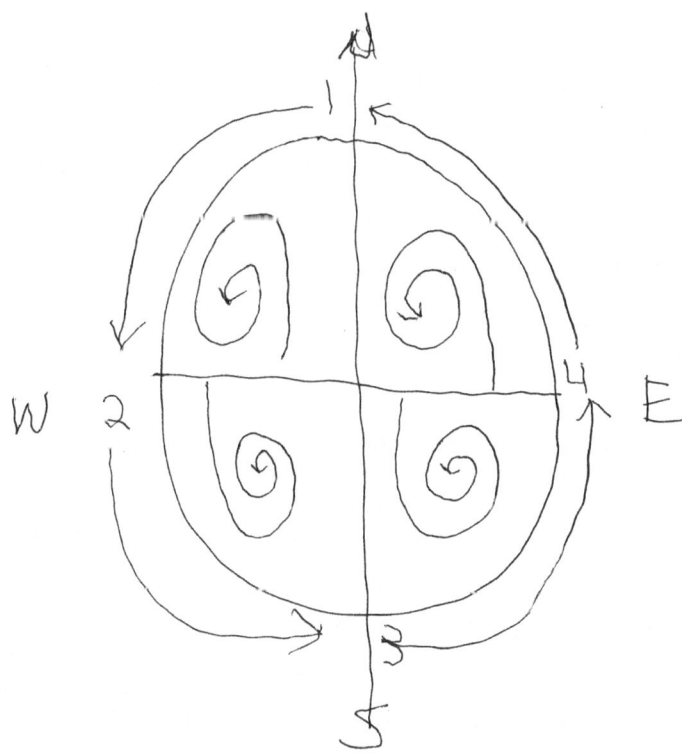

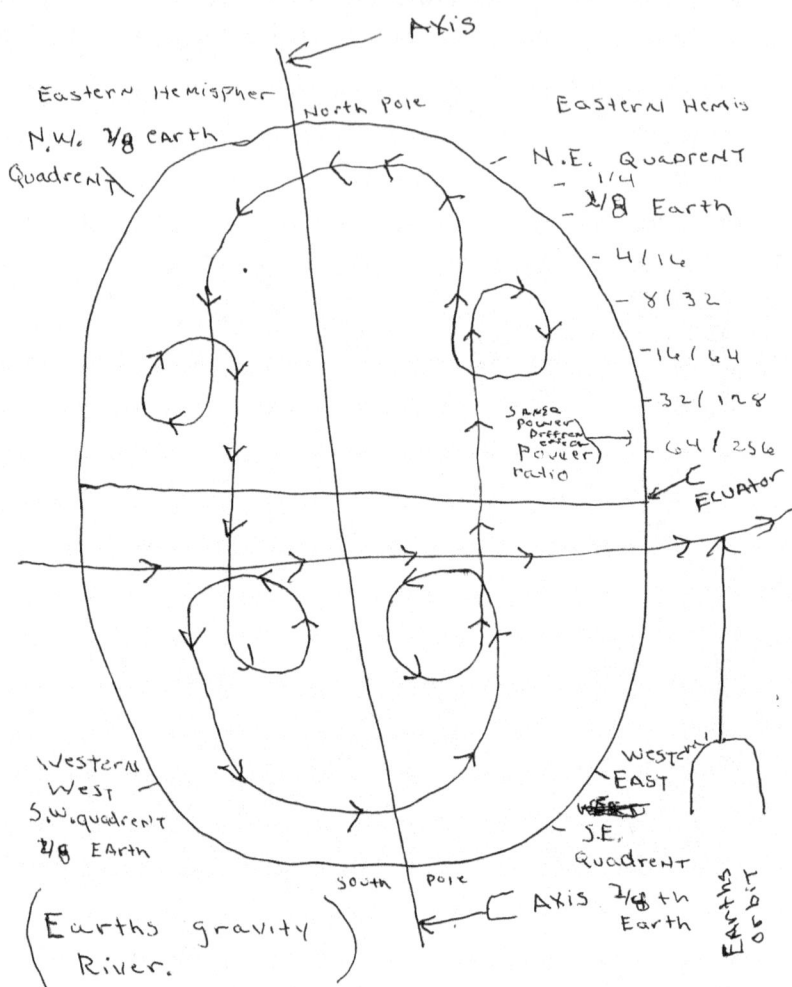

mind.

Currents have a different process. Then waves same cause different effect.

As energy moves up through the water column, it receives less tension from the sea bottom and more influence from the sea's surface tension.

So energy goes from being pushed to being pulled. It is at this juncture that the wind comes into effect.

The stronger the surface tension, the larger the force that caused it. Translation: The bigger the storm, the more surface tension of the ocean.

What we can take from this scenario is surface tension of the ocean con-

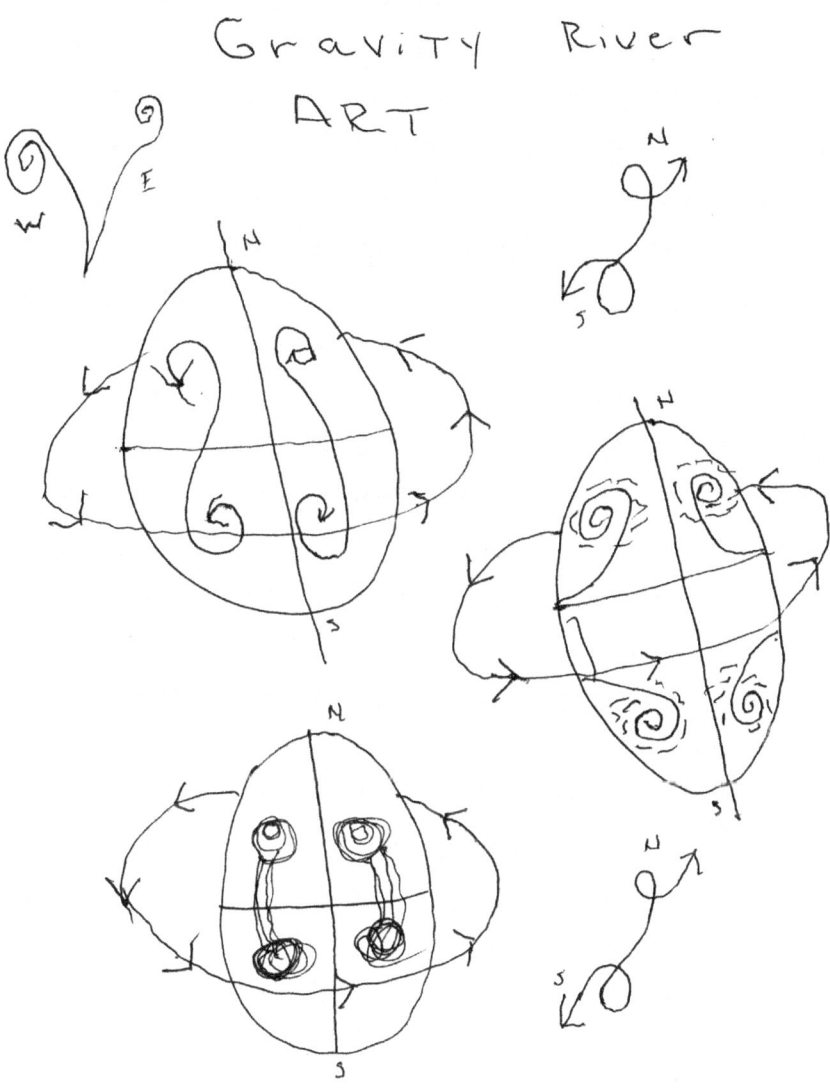

Gravity River
ART

stantly changes.

Currents are actually moved by the large negative polarity of the continents. Not just wind.

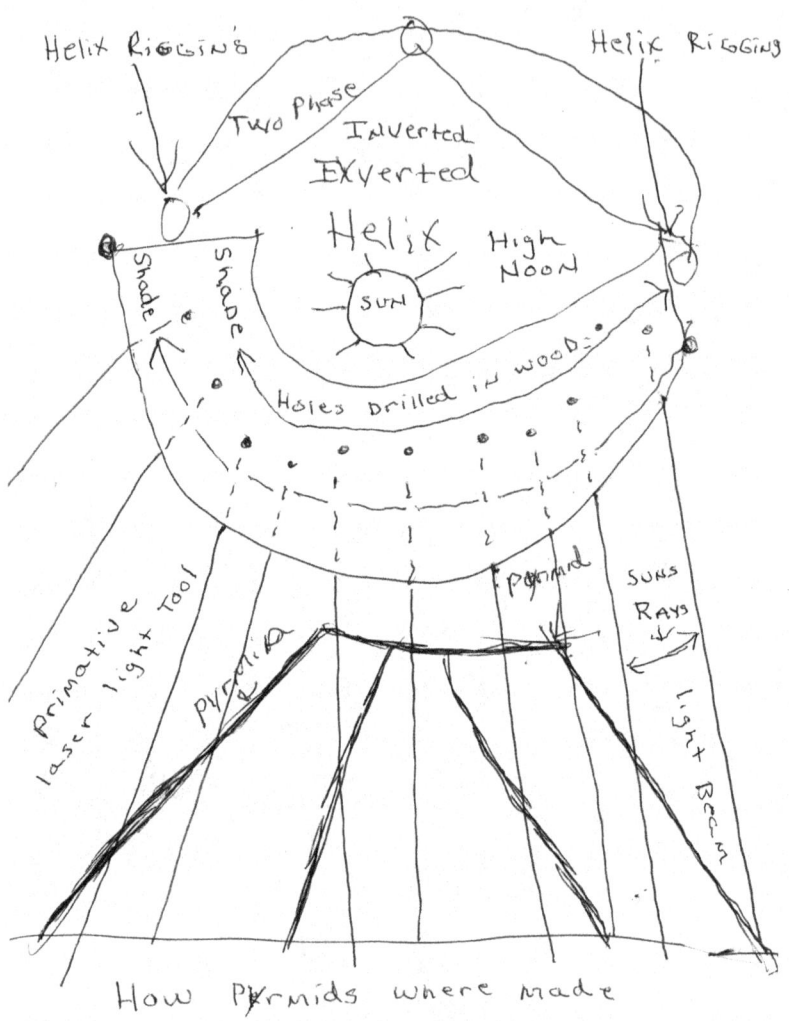

How Pyrmids where made

As well as the ocean's large magnetic push.

As Earth's orbit/minute of angle turns, you will notice that the main current flows switch direction.

The North American continent has a larger effect on the current because of the shape of the land mass.

A huge fact that seems not to have come up is they effect that the Eastern Hemisphere has on the Western Hemisphere's main currents.

They repeal and retract one another. The currents on one side of the

Earth push and pull the currents on the other side of the Earth. So we have an element of perpetual motion in play. As well sun, moon, and wind. It almost has the functionality of an electrical fan.

As we approach the sun in orbit, the effect is intensified by the Earth's expansion. This is hurricane season. The result is a larger storm surge. Increased wind speed.

If you follow flow charts of both hemispheres, you will find them to be the same. They mimic Earth's rotation. The only difference being the shape of the continents on each hemisphere, shapes, and contours the flows.

Currents in the oceans are affected at the same rate as those of the continents. The difference is the amount of surface tension in the continent is a lot stronger. If you want to see the force of a storm on a continent, you look to the ocean. It's the same force.

GRAVITY FORMULA

If you take all the magnetic material in the Earth, then add all the magnetic material together, you will get a gross force of magnetic energy for the planet.

Here are the mechanics behind the process, even though the magnetic materials are on the planet.

The force of the magnetic material extends all the way to the edge of our atmosphere.

It is at this point that magnetic force is lost. So no gravity can exist beyond this perimeter. Atoms lose the ability to bond without magnetic influence. Our atmosphere ends where Earth's magnetic capabilities end.

Gravity has two separate functions. And the mechanics of those two functions employ different techniques.

Gravity Theory
(Soft Bond Gravity)

When low heat and slow velocity and short distances are traveled, soft bond gravity is the primary force.

Magnetic properties acting on other magnetic properties with the same force as the force it controls.

Soft bond gravity is a two phase gravity.

Force of gravity

X force of object

To calculate the force of gravity.

Multiply

Object in its entirety
X velocity of object
X distance traveled by object
X Arc 3 = force of gravity to stop object

Math Formula
OE x VO x DTO x Arc 3 = gF

10 lb object x 10 mph velocity x 10 feet distance traveled = Arc 3
10 OE x 10 VO = 100 x 10 DT = 1000 x Arc 3 = 2000 FT pounds of gravity.

A ten-pound object traveling ten miles an hour for ten feet will create 1000 ft pounds of pressure. 1000 to match 1000 to stop.

Add the 2000 ft pounds of gravity it would take to stop the object.

Combine both numbers together. And you get 3000 ft pounds of pressure created by an object. A ton-half of pressure to stop the object.

Once the object is stopped, the object's energy as well as gravity's energy reverts back to magnetic energy. A preset number based on the total magnetic weight of Earth.

(Hot Bond Gravity)

Hot Bond Gravity is the mechanical solution for dealing with nuclear temperatures, extreme velocities stopping in very short distances.

If magnetic energy gets too hot, the energy will explode into nuclear fission. Gravity has a heat transfer process to keep this from happening.
Example:

An asteroid crashes into Earth's atmosphere.

Gravity is there to meet the asteroid head on.

As the gravity and asteroid collide, the temperature instantly rises to nuclear fission levels.

Now remember, magnetic energy burns up if it gets too hot. So gravity calls in for reinforcement.

As the meteorite travels through magnetic gravity, sparks of electricity start to fly off of the meteorite.

Next a giant light appears, followed by a weird echoic sound.

(Heat Continuum Process)

Magnetic energy heats up, turns excess energy to electrical waves.

Electrical waves turn the heat into light waves.

Light waves turn the heat into sound waves.

Now that heat is diminished, sound waves convert back to magnetic wave.

Five-dimensional transfer of gravity. Back to predetermined strength based on the total magnetic force of Earth.

Five-Dimensional Gravity

1) Magnetic force
2) Electric force
3) Light force
4) Sound force
5) Back to magnetic force, 5th power

To calculate the force of hot bond gravity, you only count the powers that transferred energy from gravity.

Remember, magnetic gravity is a constant.

To get the force of the asteroid, use your new gravity formula.

Multiply

Force of electrical sparks

X force of light waves

X force of sound waves

= force of gravity displaced

Now take force of asteroid by multiplying

Asteroid in its entirety

X velocity traveled in gravity

X distance traveled in gravity

= force of gravitational disruption caused by asteroid

These two formulas offset one another and restore gravity back to normal magnetic force.

That's why you exclude magnetic energy in calculations. You return back to magnetic zero. Pre-calculated number.

The energy follows a three-dimensional heat profile to return to its original state. Kind of a "here I am, there I go" scenario.
Gravity River Theory

The moon creates the Earth's axis. The axis creates the Earth's slant. The orbit creates the Earth's movement. And the oceans' waters create perpetual motion = Gravity River.

Eighty-eight is the natural flow pattern you get from the gravity river when you combine the four main quadrants of Earth.

A force, created by a force, to control a force. Three-dimensional manipulation.

Virus Theory

Viruses = are the next genetic link in species formation.

Unable to develop mode of travel at such an early stage of development.

Viruses perform in the same mechanical function as a parasitic would, only lacking a body. Unlike a flea, a virus is a parasitic on the inside, using the host's ability to feed, generate heat, and provide plenty of electromagnetic current. And also gain mobility to travel.

A virus has gained a foothold into genetic mutation after thousands of years. Viruses now live aboveground and have their own endro-system, full functional skeletal systems developed into a completely evolved system to host a new species. Species regeneration leads to evolved adaptation.

Bacterium Theory

Bacterium are viruses in formation. The bacterium has not developed to the level of functioning with a live host. So they compromise and feed on dead and dying hosts by attacking the cellular composition of compromised hosts, operating on the same mechanical function as a flock of buzzards on your insides. Symbiotic digestion when hosts perish. They work their way from inside to outside. Cancerous feeding vermin. Creating a new evolved species out of the demise of the old species. Energy reabsorption. What one calls foul, another calls dinner. Bacteria are not picky eaters. They don't taste, smell, or breathe. Their only function is to absorb energy. They just steal the mitochondria DNA from their hosts. Absorption leading to advanced genetic species.

Dissimilation/Reassemlation Theory
(Nuclear Bomb)

Uses magnetic material, plutonium, or uranium.

Detonator = battery runs electrical pulses through magnets. The enriched plutonium explodes.

This explosion is the dissimilation of periodicals, elements returning back to their original state.

The process of elements returning to an original state is reassimilation. Nature returning to its state of entirety.

When an outside force is stronger than an internal force, gravity makes the correction. Energy is the result of reassimilation, not dissimulation. In dissimulation, energy is lost.

Storm Theory

There are two stages of a storm.

(stage 1)

Internal stage: Force of storm is controlled by ground force, which is controlled by core force.

(stage 2)

External stage: When force of storm exits Earth's crust.

Storms are the result of nuclear fission taking place in the Earth's core. As energy passes through Earth's mantle, nuclear fusion takes place.

When the energy comes into contact with Earth's periodicals, the extreme heat turns these materials into volcanic lava, depending on the thermal intensity of a storm.

A number of different compounds can be produced, from hard bond compounds to soft bond compounds.

An example of a hard bond compound is a diamond. All gems can be said to be hard bond compounds.

Medium bond= compound is our precious metals, gold and silver.

A light bond compound = limestone.

Remember, the force of the storm controls the complexity of the compounds produced.

Hot = more complex

Cooler = less complex

We're talking nuclear fusion here, so even soft bond materials are thousands of degrees. But thermal fluctuation is key to compound varieties.

There are a couple of other forces involved in the determination of compound composure.

Hard bond compounds can only be gotten from mining. Since the compounds are deep underground, the constant force of Earth's pressure compacts the compounds, turning them very hard.

Located between the upper layers of the crust are the precious medals. Reduced amounts of Earth's pressure cause a softer bond.

These precious metals can migrate to the Earth's surface through the process of creek and river erosion.

Soft compounds are the ones found on the Earth's surface, lacking the force of Earth's force.

In addition to being exposed to the Earth's surface, wind, and rain, these compounds cool quicker. That's the reason for the softer bond. They're out in the elements.

Now let's take a break from conventional thought. Let's step all the way to the edge of the limb. Just don't fall off.

Now, if we all are in agreement here, the core is a giant chemistry set responsible for the elements and compounds of our planet, which I believe is a common-held belief.

Science tells us the bonding of materials is fusion. Now either you can agree or disagree with that statement.

I'm not here to make that determination for you. What you personally believe is and always will be your business.

By this point, some of you will have already guessed where I'm going with this. So I'm ready to throw my cards in.

If the Earth has the ability to create all forms of compounds, why would it not have the ability to create species as well?

Change the chemistry a bit. Add some antigens and a little protein, pre-encoded DNA, get the picture yet?

Plant, animals, all core function. Core is the nucleus of a planet. Central distribution center. Twenty-four hours a day, seven days a week, times billions of years, always on the job. Go core.

Now where does lifeform develop? We don't see it. Simple life energy develops in the oil of the vast underground lakes and caverns.

Think of the oil as the amniotic fluid: nice, warm, and full of magnetic and electrical pulse waves. A great place for DNA to flourish.

In the oil, species could grow free of airborne pathogens. That could destroy the DNA before it ever got started. In the oil, the proteins required for propagation would be in a sterilized environment, free from air, water, mold, and mycelium infections.

It basically performs the same function as an umbilical sack does in primates.

As I've stated before, we are a replication of a replication, and species need to be protected at this stage of development. So in reality, the storms we experience are Earth's equivalent of labor pains.

Life-forming energy going through its cycles. A constant transfer of energies.

The ranking of storms in strength that the core creates, either directly or indirectly.

1) Nuclear explosion/dissimilation
2) Volcano eruption
3) Tsunami
4) Hurricane
5) Tornado
6) Lightning storm
7) Hail
8) Downpour
9) Rain
10) Mist
11) Fog *All mechanics from core
12) Wind energy
13) Riptide
14) Undertow
15) Rapid
16) Wave
17) Tidal
18) Ripple
19) Eddy
20) Trace
21) Drop
22) Molecule

23) Refraction
24) Rainbow

Storms/Theory
(Recipe for Storm)

A) Storms are they result of nuclear fission taking place in the Earth's core.
B) As pressure in the core builds, it transfers the energy into fusion.
C) That pressure travels through the Earth's crust. Energy is transferred into large explosions in volcanic activity and earthquakes. That's how it works on the continents.
D) Same principal for the sea floor. As pressure rises through the water, water starts to osculate.
E) This in turn spawns transfers of energy, riptides, tidal waves, and tsunamis. All forms of water waves, some having shallow water reaction, others deep water reaction.
F) As the energy exits the Earth's crust, the negative-charged forces bond with the positive forces of environment.
G) The negative forces also bond with the positive forces over the surfaces of all bodies of water.
H) Those energy forces in turn start to rise into the atmosphere. As they energy rises, it starts to osculate.

Storms Continued

A) Represent pre-storm positive/negative/osculation

Storms Continued

A) As the particles mix with warm air, a full storm occurs.

Storms Continued

A) The recipe for a storm. The larger the nuclear reaction in the Earth's core, the larger the storm.
B) The severity of the force can be measured in the amount and force of lightning strikes.
C) If you combined all the lightning strikes in a storm from beginning to end, record their force, and add them all together, it would tell you the strength of the storm.
D) That information should be able to come from a satellite.

Storms Continued

A) As the storm climbs higher, the oxygen gets thinner. The heat starts to reside, and the storm is eventually absorbed back into the atmosphere.

B) Storms also have the ability to mix together. Hurricanes and tornadoes are the result of this combination. One if by land, two if by sea.

www.ingramcontent.com/pod-product-compliance
Lightning Source LLC
Chambersburg PA
CBHW070511290526
45790CB00003B/1185